Y0-CJC-948

Fun with Abby & Alyssa ™

An Introduction to Sign Language

A day with our Family

Written by Grandpa Don
Illustrated by Liam Gooley

Written by Grandpa Don
Illustrated by Liam Gooley

Fun With Abby and Alyssa
A day with our Family
Copyright @ 2011 by Donald McNamara

Illustrations Copyright @ 2011 by Donald McNamara

All rights reserved.This book may not be reproduced, transmitted or stored in whole or in part by any means, including graphic, electronic, or mechanical without the express written consent of Donald McNamara except in the case of brief quotations embodied in critical articles and reviews.

ISBN#: 978-0-9833163-3-6

Dedication

Abby and Alyssa are real people. They both have significant medical challenges and use sign language to talk. As growing sisters, their energy and charisma can be inspirational to anyone that wishes to learn.

This series of books is dedicated to Abby and Alyssa who inspire me, and to Grandma Gina who lives on within our hearts.

Grandpa Don

Hi! My name is Abby and this is my sister Alyssa.

Alyssa uses signs instead of words to talk. She makes these signs with her hands.

You already know some signs like waving your hand to say hi.

Come with us to meet our family and we'll learn more signs!

Hi: Open hand waved side to side.

There are signs for many things like "family".

Let's see who in the family we can find and sign them together!

Family: "F" sign both hands, index fingers touching in front of chest, palms facing each other, bring hands away from each other in small arc until fingers touch.

Who is that person?

The Sign: Tap the thumb of the right "5" hand, palm facing left, against the chin twice.

That's right, she's Mommy!

Let's all make the sign for Mommy!

Mommy: Tap the thumb of the right "5" hand, palm facing left, against the chin twice.

Who is with Mommy?

The Sign: Tap the thumb of the right "5" hand, palm facing left, against the forehead twice.

Let's all make the sign for Daddy!

Daddy: Tap the thumb of the right "5" hand, palm facing left, against the forehead twice.

This is Avery.
Who is she?

The Sign: Move the thumb of the right "A" hand down right cheek. Then tap the index fingers of "1" hands together in front of body.

That's right,
Avery is our sister!

Let's all make the sign for sister!

Sister: Move the thumb of the right "A" hand down right cheek. Then tap the index fingers of "1" hands together in front of body.

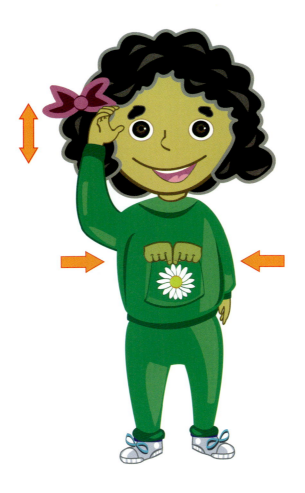

The Sign: Begining with the index finger of the right "C" hand near the right side of the forehead, palm facing left, close the fingers twice. Then tap the index fingers of "1" hands together in front of body.

Let's all make the sign for brother!

Brother: Begining with the index finger of the right "C" hand near the right side of the forehead, palm facing left, close the fingers twice. Then tap the index fingers of "1" hands together in front of body.

The Sign: Touch the thumb of the right "5" hand on the forehead, palm facing left, move the hand forward in a double arc.

Let's all make the sign for Grandpa!

Grandpa: Touch the thumb of the right "5" hand on the forehead, palm facing left, move the hand forward in a double arc.

Who is with Grandpa?

The Sign: Touch the thumb of the right "5" hand on the chin, palm facing left, then move hand forward in a double arc.

Let's all make the sign for Grandma!

Grandma: Touch the thumb of the right "5" hand on the chin, palm facing left, then move hand forward in a double arc.

We've learned the signs for our family today.

It's time for Alyssa and me to go home...

Let's all make the sign for good-bye!

Good-Bye: Wave open hand up and down.

For more fun with sign language, you can practice your A,B,C's and numbers!

alphabet

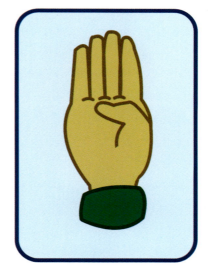

A   **B**

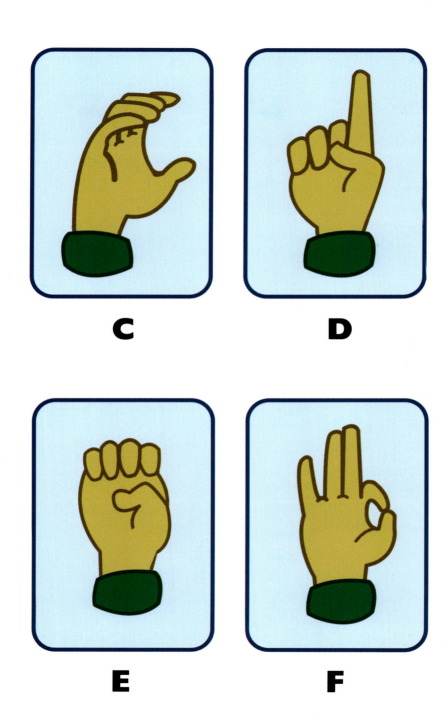

C

D

E

F

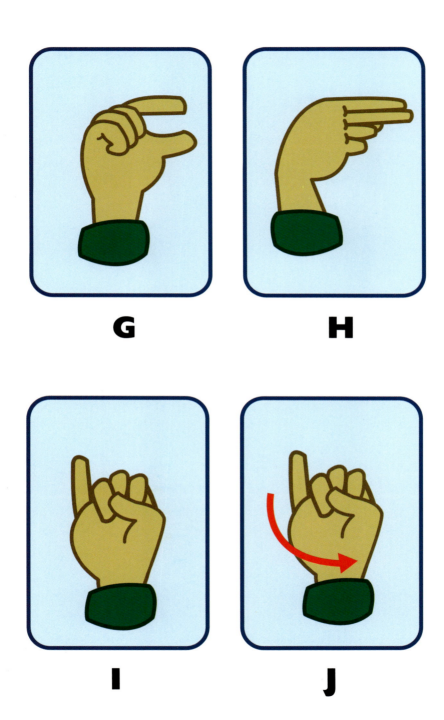

G

H

I

J

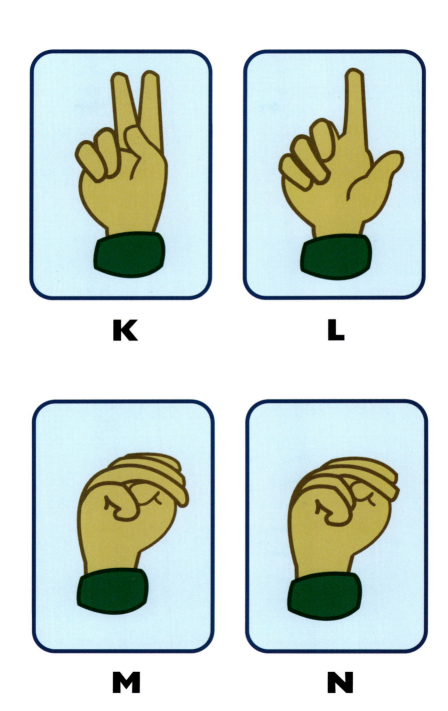

K L

M N

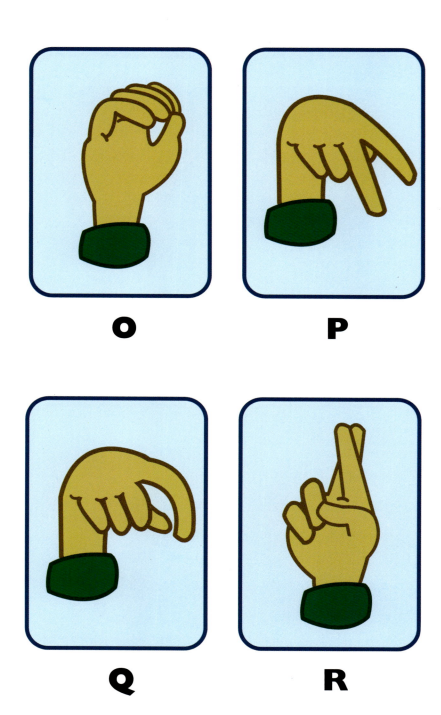

O

P

Q

R

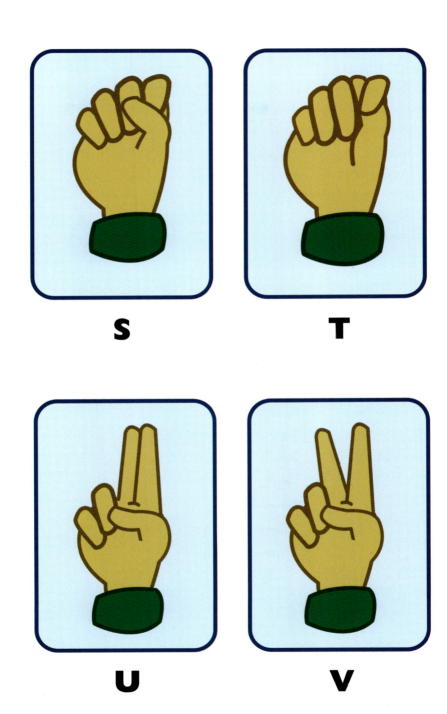

S

T

U

V

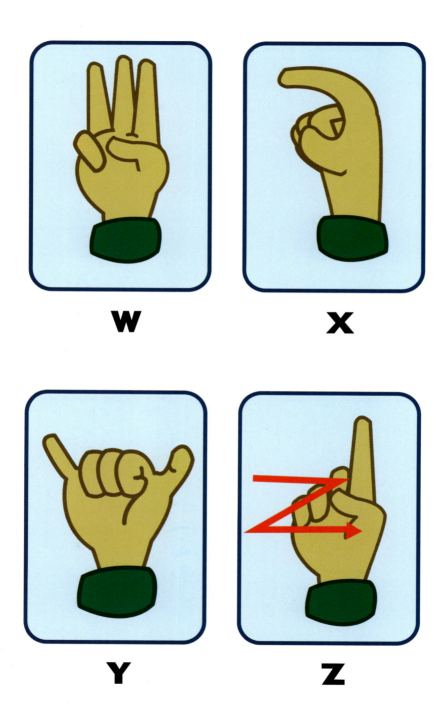

W

X

Y

Z

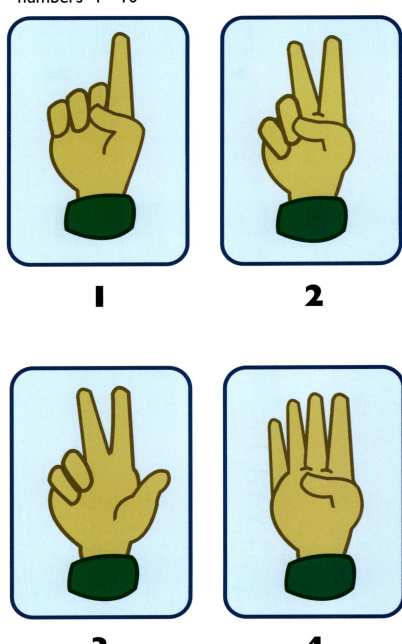

1

2

3

4

5

6

7

8

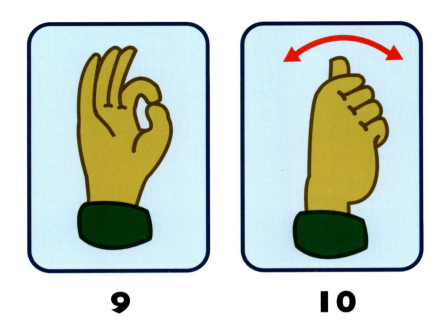

9 10

Acknowledgements

Some words in sign language have multiple acceptable signs. In those instances where multiple signs were available, Grandpa Don chose the sign most appropriate for Abby and Alyssa.

Grandpa Don encourages readers who want to learn more about sign language to read:

• "The Art of Sign Language" by
   Christopher Brown; Random House.

• "Webster's Unabridged American
   Sign Language Dictionary" by Elaine Costello, PHD.

And to also visit these websites:

• www.signingsavvy.com

• www.lessontutor.com